LOW CONTENT BOOK PLANNER

Brainstorm, research, and organize your next 10 low content journals, recipe books, planners, notebooks, coloring books, and more!

Diana Poisson
Find practical information about selling digital and physical products online at secondhalfdreams.com

Layout, design, and writing © 2019 Diana Poisson

All rights reserved. No part of this book may be reproduced or transmitted in any form or by any means, including but not limited to information storage and retrieval systems, electronic, mechanical, photocopy, recording, etc. without written permission from the copyright holder.

ISBN-13: 978-1-796916-25-6

Brainstorm Topics

Brainstorm low-content book ideas and check off the box once it's published. Ideas to consider are hobbies, sports, recipes, 90-day, holidays, events, goals, occupations, health, animals, inspiration, and gratitude.

- [ ] _____
- [ ] _____
- [ ] _____
- [ ] _____
- [ ] _____
- [ ] _____
- [ ] _____
- [ ] _____
- [ ] _____
- [ ] _____
- [ ] _____
- [ ] _____
- [ ] _____
- [ ] _____
- [ ] _____
- [ ] _____
- [ ] _____
- [ ] _____
- [ ] _____
- [ ] _____
- [ ] _____
- [ ] _____
- [ ] _____

Brainstorm Topics

Brainstorm low-content book ideas and check off the box once it's published. Ideas to consider are hobbies, sports, recipes, 90-day, holidays, events, goals, occupations, health, animals, inspiration, and gratitude.

- ☐ _____
- ☐ _____
- ☐ _____
- ☐ _____
- ☐ _____
- ☐ _____
- ☐ _____
- ☐ _____
- ☐ _____
- ☐ _____
- ☐ _____
- ☐ _____
- ☐ _____
- ☐ _____
- ☐ _____
- ☐ _____
- ☐ _____
- ☐ _____
- ☐ _____
- ☐ _____
- ☐ _____
- ☐ _____
- ☐ _____

Book #1

As you progress through each step of your book, write down the book details for easy reference.

Book Idea: _____

Date Started: _____

Date Published: _____

File name of interior file: _____

File name of cover file: _____

Title: _____

Size: _____ # Pages: _____

ISBN: _____

Printer: _____

Cost: _____ Selling Price: _____

Primary Font & Size: _____

Secondary Font & Size: _____

Accent Font & Size: _____

Primary Cover Color: _____

Secondary Cover Color: _____

Cover Image Source: _____

Cover Image Credit: _____

Keyword Research

Write down your criteria for validating keywords.
Examples are Monthly Search Volume > 5,000 and Number of Competing Products < 3,000.

Keyword Research

Make a list of the keywords & phrases that you'll be targeting.

Customer Reviews

Read the customer reviews of the competing products. Write down what people liked and didn't like:

What people liked:

1. _____
2. _____
3. _____
4. _____
5. _____
6. _____
7. _____
8. _____
9. _____
10. _____

What people didn't like:

1. _____
2. _____
3. _____
4. _____
5. _____
6. _____
7. _____
8. _____
9. _____
10. _____

Target Audience

My target audience:

_____
_____
_____
_____
_____
_____

Top reason why a member of my target audience will buy and write a 5-star review about my book:

_____
_____
_____
_____
_____
_____

For Bundlers -

What other products is my target audience looking for that will compliment my book?

1. _____
2. _____
3. _____
4. _____
5. _____

Book Details

Language: _____

Title: _____

Subtitle: _____

Series Name: _____ Number: _____

Edition Number: _____

Author: _____

Additional Contributor: _____ Role: _____

Publishing Rights: ❑ I own the copyright   ❑ This is a public domain work

Category 1: _____

Category 2: _____

Adult Content: ❑ Yes   ❑ No

Book Details

Keywords:

_____
_____
_____
_____
_____
_____

Description:

_____
_____
_____
_____
_____
_____
_____
_____
_____
_____
_____
_____
_____
_____

Book Details

Continue your book description, write your back cover description or write additional notes.

Book Details

ISBN: ❏ Free KDP ISBN   ❏ Use my own ISBN

ISBN Number: _____

Publication Date: _____

Print Options: ❏ B & W Interior Cream Paper   ❏ B & W White Paper
                 ❏ Color Interior
                 ❏ Other: _____

Trim Size:_____

Bleed Settings: ❏ No Bleed   ❏ Bleed

Cover Finish: ❏ Matte   ❏ Glossy

List other book details below:

_____
_____
_____
_____
_____
_____
_____

Interior Layout

Think about your book pages and the elements that they will include.

Examples:
- Copyright Page
- Title Page
- Pages with blank lines, dot grids, and doodling boxes.
- Blank recipe pages
- To-Do list with check boxes
- Coloring page with a flower
- Log page with table to record dates and readings
- Daily, weekly, monthly or annual calendar
- Goal-tracking page with an inspirational quote
- Writing prompts
- Advertising page for my other books/website

My book will include:

_____
_____
_____
_____
_____
_____
_____
_____
_____
_____

Visual Interior Layout

Sketch the interior pages of your book.

Inside Front Cover	**Page 1**
Page 2	**Page 3**
Page 4	**Page 5**

Visual Interior Layout

Sketch the interior pages of your book.

Page 6	Page 7
Page 8	Page 9
Page 10	Page 11

Visual Interior Layout

Sketch the interior pages of your book.

Page 12	Page 13
Page 14	Page 15
Page 16	Page 17

Visual Interior Layout

Sketch the interior pages of your book.

Page 18	Page 19
Page 20	Page 21
Page 22	Page 23

Visual Interior Layout

Sketch the interior pages of your book.

Page 24	Page 25
Page 26	Page 27
Page 28	Page 29

Back Cover

Use this page to sketch your back cover design.

Front Cover

Use this page to sketch your front cover design.

Congratulations!!

You finished your low content book!

Book #2

As you progress through each step of your book, write down the book details for easy reference.

Book Idea: _____

Date Started: _____

Date Published: _____

File name of interior file: _____

File name of cover file: _____

Title: _____

Size: _____ # Pages: _____

ISBN: _____

Printer: _____

Cost: _____ Selling Price: _____

Primary Font & Size: _____

Secondary Font & Size: _____

Accent Font & Size: _____

Primary Cover Color: _____

Secondary Cover Color: _____

Cover Image Source: _____

Cover Image Credit: _____

Keyword Research

Write down your criteria for validating keywords.
Examples are Monthly Search Volume > 5,000 and Number of Competing Products < 3,000.

Keyword Research

Make a list of the keywords & phrases that you'll be targeting.

_____
_____
_____
_____
_____
_____
_____
_____
_____
_____
_____
_____
_____
_____
_____
_____
_____
_____
_____
_____
_____
_____
_____
_____
_____

Customer Reviews

Read the customer reviews of the competing products. Write down what people liked and didn't like:

What people liked:

1. _____
2. _____
3. _____
4. _____
5. _____
6. _____
7. _____
8. _____
9. _____
10. _____

What people didn't like:

1. _____
2. _____
3. _____
4. _____
5. _____
6. _____
7. _____
8. _____
9. _____
10. _____

Target Audience

My target audience:

_____
_____
_____
_____
_____
_____

Top reason why a member of my target audience will buy and write a 5-star review about my book:

_____
_____
_____
_____
_____
_____

For Bundlers -

What other products is my target audience looking for that will compliment my book?

1. _____
2. _____
3. _____
4. _____
5. _____

Book Details

Language: _____

Title: _____

Subtitle: _____

Series Name: _____ Number: _____

Edition Number: _____

Author: _____

Additional Contributor: _____ Role: _____

Publishing Rights: ❏ I own the copyright   ❏ This is a public domain work

Category 1: _____

Category 2: _____

Adult Content: ❏ Yes   ❏ No

Book Details

Keywords:

_____
_____
_____
_____
_____
_____
_____

Description:

_____
_____
_____
_____
_____
_____
_____
_____
_____
_____
_____
_____
_____
_____

Book Details

Continue your book description, write your back cover description or write additional notes.

Book Details

ISBN: ❏ Free KDP ISBN   ❏ Use my own ISBN

ISBN Number: _____

Publication Date: _____

Print Options: ❏ B & W Interior Cream Paper   ❏ B & W White Paper
                    ❏ Color Interior
                    ❏ Other: _____

Trim Size: _____

Bleed Settings: ❏ No Bleed   ❏ Bleed

Cover Finish: ❏ Matte   ❏ Glossy

List other book details below:

_____
_____
_____
_____
_____
_____
_____

Interior Layout

Think about your book pages and the elements that they will include.

Examples:
- Copyright Page
- Title Page
- Pages with blank lines, dot grids, and doodling boxes.
- Blank recipe pages
- To-Do list with check boxes
- Coloring page with a flower
- Log page with table to record dates and readings
- Daily, weekly, monthly or annual calendar
- Goal-tracking page with an inspirational quote
- Writing prompts
- Advertising page for my other books/website

My book will include:

_____
_____
_____
_____
_____
_____
_____
_____
_____

Visual Interior Layout

Sketch the interior pages of your book.

Inside Front Cover	**Page 1**
Page 2	**Page 3**
Page 4	**Page 5**

Visual Interior Layout

Sketch the interior pages of your book.

Page 6	Page 7
Page 8	**Page 9**
Page 10	**Page 11**

Visual Interior Layout

Sketch the interior pages of your book.

Page 12	Page 13
Page 14	Page 15
Page 16	Page 17

Visual Interior Layout

Sketch the interior pages of your book.

Page 18	Page 19
Page 20	Page 21
Page 22	Page 23

Visual Interior Layout

Sketch the interior pages of your book.

Page 24	Page 25
Page 26	Page 27
Page 28	Page 29

Back Cover

Use this page to sketch your back cover design.

Front Cover

Use this page to sketch your front cover design.

Congratulations!!

You finished your low content book!

Book #3

As you progress through each step of your book, write down the book details for easy reference.

Book Idea: _____

Date Started: _____

Date Published: _____

File name of interior file: _____

File name of cover file: _____

Title: _____

Size: _____ # Pages: _____

ISBN: _____

Printer: _____

Cost: _____ Selling Price: _____

Primary Font & Size: _____

Secondary Font & Size: _____

Accent Font & Size: _____

Primary Cover Color: _____

Secondary Cover Color: _____

Cover Image Source: _____

Cover Image Credit: _____

Keyword Research

Write down your criteria for validating keywords.
Examples are Monthly Search Volume > 5,000 and Number of Competing Products < 3,000.

Keyword Research

Make a list of the keywords & phrases that you'll be targeting.

_____
_____
_____
_____
_____
_____
_____
_____
_____
_____
_____
_____
_____
_____
_____
_____
_____
_____
_____
_____
_____
_____
_____
_____
_____

Customer Reviews

Read the customer reviews of the competing products. Write down what people liked and didn't like:

What people liked:

1. _____
2. _____
3. _____
4. _____
5. _____
6. _____
7. _____
8. _____
9. _____
10. _____

What people didn't like:

1. _____
2. _____
3. _____
4. _____
5. _____
6. _____
7. _____
8. _____
9. _____
10. _____

Target Audience

My target audience:

_____
_____
_____
_____
_____
_____
_____

Top reason why a member of my target audience will buy and write a 5-star review about my book:

_____
_____
_____
_____
_____
_____
_____

For Bundlers -

What other products is my target audience looking for that will compliment my book?

1. _____
2. _____
3. _____
4. _____
5. _____

Book Details

Language: _____

Title: _____

Subtitle: _____

Series Name: _____ Number: _____

Edition Number: _____

Author: _____

Additional Contributor: _____ Role: _____

Publishing Rights: ❑ I own the copyright   ❑ This is a public domain work

Category 1: _____

Category 2: _____

Adult Content: ❑ Yes   ❑ No

Book Details

Keywords:

_____
_____
_____
_____
_____
_____
_____

Description:

_____
_____
_____
_____
_____
_____
_____
_____
_____
_____
_____
_____
_____
_____
_____

Book Details

Continue your book description, write your back cover description or write additional notes.

_____
_____
_____
_____
_____
_____
_____
_____
_____
_____
_____
_____
_____
_____
_____
_____
_____
_____
_____
_____
_____
_____
_____
_____
_____

Book Details

ISBN: ❏ Free KDP ISBN   ❏ Use my own ISBN

ISBN Number: _____

Publication Date: _____

Print Options: ❏ B & W Interior Cream Paper   ❏ B & W White Paper
                ❏ Color Interior
                ❏ Other: _____

Trim Size: _____

Bleed Settings: ❏ No Bleed   ❏ Bleed

Cover Finish: ❏ Matte   ❏ Glossy

List other book details below:

_____
_____
_____
_____
_____
_____
_____

Interior Layout

Think about your book pages and the elements that they will include.

Examples:
- Copyright Page
- Title Page
- Pages with blank lines, dot grids, and doodling boxes.
- Blank recipe pages
- To-Do list with check boxes
- Coloring page with a flower
- Log page with table to record dates and readings
- Daily, weekly, monthly or annual calendar
- Goal-tracking page with an inspirational quote
- Writing prompts
- Advertising page for my other books/website

My book will include:

_____
_____
_____
_____
_____
_____
_____
_____
_____
_____

Visual Interior Layout

Sketch the interior pages of your book.

Inside Front Cover	Page 1
Page 2	**Page 3**
Page 4	**Page 5**

Visual Interior Layout

Sketch the interior pages of your book.

Page 6	Page 7
Page 8	Page 9
Page 10	Page 11

Visual Interior Layout

Sketch the interior pages of your book.

Page 12	Page 13
Page 14	Page 15
Page 16	Page 17

Visual Interior Layout

Sketch the interior pages of your book.

Page 18	Page 19
Page 20	Page 21
Page 22	Page 23

Visual Interior Layout

Sketch the interior pages of your book.

Page 24	Page 25
Page 26	Page 27
Page 28	Page 29

Back Cover

Use this page to sketch your back cover design.

Front Cover

Use this page to sketch your front cover design.

Congratulations!!

You finished your low content book!

Book #4

As you progress through each step of your book, write down the book details for easy reference.

Book Idea: _____

Date Started: _____

Date Published: _____

File name of interior file: _____

File name of cover file: _____

Title: _____

Size: _____ # Pages: _____

ISBN: _____

Printer: _____

Cost: _____ Selling Price: _____

Primary Font & Size: _____

Secondary Font & Size: _____

Accent Font & Size: _____

Primary Cover Color: _____

Secondary Cover Color: _____

Cover Image Source: _____

Cover Image Credit: _____

Keyword Research

Write down your criteria for validating keywords.
Examples are Monthly Search Volume > 5,000 and Number of Competing Products < 3,000.

Keyword Research

Make a list of the keywords & phrases that you'll be targeting.

Customer Reviews

Read the customer reviews of the competing products. Write down what people liked and didn't like:

What people liked:

1. _____
2. _____
3. _____
4. _____
5. _____
6. _____
7. _____
8. _____
9. _____
10. _____

What people didn't like:

1. _____
2. _____
3. _____
4. _____
5. _____
6. _____
7. _____
8. _____
9. _____
10. _____

Target Audience

My target audience:

_____
_____
_____
_____
_____
_____

Top reason why a member of my target audience will buy and write a 5-star review about my book:

_____
_____
_____
_____
_____
_____

For Bundlers -

What other products is my target audience looking for that will compliment my book?

1. _____
2. _____
3. _____
4. _____
5. _____

Book Details

Language: _____

Title: _____

Subtitle: _____

Series Name: _____ Number: _____

Edition Number: _____

Author: _____

Additional Contributor: _____ Role: _____

Publishing Rights: ❏ I own the copyright   ❏ This is a public domain work

Category 1: _____

Category 2: _____

Adult Content: ❏ Yes   ❏ No

Book Details

Keywords:

Description:

Book Details

Continue your book description, write your back cover description or write additional notes.

___
___
___
___
___
___
___
___
___
___
___
___
___
___
___
___
___
___
___
___
___
___
___

Book Details

ISBN: ❏ Free KDP ISBN   ❏ Use my own ISBN

ISBN Number: _____

Publication Date: _____

Print Options: ❏ B & W Interior Cream Paper   ❏ B & W White Paper
　　　　　　　　❏ Color Interior
　　　　　　　　❏ Other: _____

Trim Size: _____

Bleed Settings: ❏ No Bleed   ❏ Bleed

Cover Finish: ❏ Matte   ❏ Glossy

List other book details below:

_____
_____
_____
_____
_____
_____
_____

Interior Layout

Think about your book pages and the elements that they will include.

Examples:
- Copyright Page
- Title Page
- Pages with blank lines, dot grids, and doodling boxes.
- Blank recipe pages
- To-Do list with check boxes
- Coloring page with a flower
- Log page with table to record dates and readings
- Daily, weekly, monthly or annual calendar
- Goal-tracking page with an inspirational quote
- Writing prompts
- Advertising page for my other books/website

My book will include:

_____
_____
_____
_____
_____
_____
_____
_____
_____
_____

Visual Interior Layout

Sketch the interior pages of your book.

Inside Front Cover	Page 1
Page 2	**Page 3**
Page 4	**Page 5**

Visual Interior Layout

Sketch the interior pages of your book.

Page 6	Page 7
Page 8	**Page 9**
Page 10	**Page 11**

Visual Interior Layout

Sketch the interior pages of your book.

Page 12	Page 13
Page 14	Page 15
Page 16	Page 17

Visual Interior Layout

Sketch the interior pages of your book.

Page 18	Page 19
Page 20	Page 21
Page 22	Page 23

Visual Interior Layout

Sketch the interior pages of your book.

Page 24	**Page 25**
Page 26	**Page 27**
Page 28	**Page 29**

Back Cover

Use this page to sketch your back cover design.

Front Cover

Use this page to sketch your front cover design.

Congratulations!!

You finished your low content book!

Book #5

As you progress through each step of your book, write down the book details for easy reference.

Book Idea: _____

Date Started: _____

Date Published: _____

File name of interior file: _____

File name of cover file: _____

Title: _____

Size: _____ # Pages: _____

ISBN: _____

Printer: _____

Cost: _____ Selling Price: _____

Primary Font & Size: _____

Secondary Font & Size: _____

Accent Font & Size: _____

Primary Cover Color: _____

Secondary Cover Color: _____

Cover Image Source: _____

Cover Image Credit: _____

Keyword Research

Write down your criteria for validating keywords.
Examples are Monthly Search Volume > 5,000 and Number of Competing Products < 3,000.

Keyword Research

Make a list of the keywords & phrases that you'll be targeting.

_____
_____
_____
_____
_____
_____
_____
_____
_____
_____
_____
_____
_____
_____
_____
_____
_____
_____
_____
_____
_____
_____
_____
_____

Customer Reviews

Read the customer reviews of the competing products. Write down what people liked and didn't like:

What people liked:

1. _____
2. _____
3. _____
4. _____
5. _____
6. _____
7. _____
8. _____
9. _____
10. _____

What people didn't like:

1. _____
2. _____
3. _____
4. _____
5. _____
6. _____
7. _____
8. _____
9. _____
10. _____

Target Audience

My target audience:

_____
_____
_____
_____
_____
_____

Top reason why a member of my target audience will buy and write a 5-star review about my book:

_____
_____
_____
_____
_____
_____

For Bundlers -

What other products is my target audience looking for that will compliment my book?

1. _____
2. _____
3. _____
4. _____
5. _____

Book Details

Language: _____

Title: _____

Subtitle: _____

Series Name: _____ Number: _____

Edition Number: _____

Author: _____

Additional Contributor: _____ Role: _____

Publishing Rights: ❏ I own the copyright   ❏ This is a public domain work

Category 1: _____

Category 2: _____

Adult Content: ❏ Yes   ❏ No

Book Details

Keywords:

Description:

Book Details

Continue your book description, write your back cover description or write additional notes.

_____
_____
_____
_____
_____
_____
_____
_____
_____
_____
_____
_____
_____
_____
_____
_____
_____
_____
_____
_____
_____
_____
_____

Book Details

ISBN: ❏ Free KDP ISBN   ❏ Use my own ISBN

ISBN Number: _____

Publication Date: _____

Print Options: ❏ B & W Interior Cream Paper   ❏ B & W White Paper
❏ Color Interior
❏ Other: _____

Trim Size: _____

Bleed Settings: ❏ No Bleed   ❏ Bleed

Cover Finish: ❏ Matte   ❏ Glossy

List other book details below:

_____
_____
_____
_____
_____
_____
_____

Interior Layout

Think about your book pages and the elements that they will include.

Examples:
- Copyright Page
- Title Page
- Pages with blank lines, dot grids, and doodling boxes.
- Blank recipe pages
- To-Do list with check boxes
- Coloring page with a flower
- Log page with table to record dates and readings
- Daily, weekly, monthly or annual calendar
- Goal-tracking page with an inspirational quote
- Writing prompts
- Advertising page for my other books/website

My book will include:

_____
_____
_____
_____
_____
_____
_____
_____
_____
_____

Visual Interior Layout

Sketch the interior pages of your book.

Inside Front Cover	**Page 1**
Page 2	**Page 3**
Page 4	**Page 5**

Visual Interior Layout

Sketch the interior pages of your book.

Page 6	Page 7
Page 8	Page 9
Page 10	Page 11

Visual Interior Layout

Sketch the interior pages of your book.

Page 12	Page 13
Page 14	Page 15
Page 16	Page 17

Visual Interior Layout

Sketch the interior pages of your book.

Page 18	Page 19
Page 20	Page 21
Page 22	Page 23

Visual Interior Layout

Sketch the interior pages of your book.

Page 24	Page 25
Page 26	Page 27
Page 28	Page 29

Back Cover

Use this page to sketch your back cover design.

Front Cover

Use this page to sketch your front cover design.

Congratulations!!

You finished your low content book!

Book #6

As you progress through each step of your book, write down the book details for easy reference.

Book Idea: _____

Date Started: _____

Date Published: _____

File name of interior file: _____

File name of cover file: _____

Title: _____

Size: _____ # Pages: _____

ISBN: _____

Printer: _____

Cost: _____ Selling Price: _____

Primary Font & Size: _____

Secondary Font & Size: _____

Accent Font & Size: _____

Primary Cover Color: _____

Secondary Cover Color: _____

Cover Image Source: _____

Cover Image Credit: _____

Keyword Research

Write down your criteria for validating keywords.
Examples are Monthly Search Volume > 5,000 and Number of Competing Products < 3,000.

Keyword Research

Make a list of the keywords & phrases that you'll be targeting.

Customer Reviews

Read the customer reviews of the competing products. Write down what people liked and didn't like:

What people liked:

1. _____
2. _____
3. _____
4. _____
5. _____
6. _____
7. _____
8. _____
9. _____
10. _____

What people didn't like:

1. _____
2. _____
3. _____
4. _____
5. _____
6. _____
7. _____
8. _____
9. _____
10. _____

Target Audience

My target audience:

_____
_____
_____
_____
_____
_____

Top reason why a member of my target audience will buy and write a 5-star review about my book:

_____
_____
_____
_____
_____
_____

For Bundlers -

What other products is my target audience looking for that will compliment my book?

1. _____
2. _____
3. _____
4. _____
5. _____

Book Details

Language: _____

Title: _____

Subtitle: _____

Series Name: _____ Number: _____

Edition Number: _____

Author: _____

Additional Contributor: _____ Role: _____

Publishing Rights: ❏ I own the copyright   ❏ This is a public domain work

Category 1: _____

Category 2: _____

Adult Content: ❏ Yes   ❏ No

Book Details

Keywords:

_____

_____

_____

_____

_____

_____

_____

Description:

_____

_____

_____

_____

_____

_____

_____

_____

_____

_____

_____

_____

_____

Book Details

Continue your book description, write your back cover description or write additional notes.

Book Details

ISBN: ❏ Free KDP ISBN   ❏ Use my own ISBN

ISBN Number: _____

Publication Date: _____

Print Options: ❏ B & W Interior Cream Paper   ❏ B & W White Paper
                 ❏ Color Interior
                 ❏ Other: _____

Trim Size: _____

Bleed Settings: ❏ No Bleed   ❏ Bleed

Cover Finish: ❏ Matte   ❏ Glossy

List other book details below:

_____
_____
_____
_____
_____
_____
_____

Interior Layout

Think about your book pages and the elements that they will include.

Examples:
- Copyright Page
- Title Page
- Pages with blank lines, dot grids, and doodling boxes.
- Blank recipe pages
- To-Do list with check boxes
- Coloring page with a flower
- Log page with table to record dates and readings
- Daily, weekly, monthly or annual calendar
- Goal-tracking page with an inspirational quote
- Writing prompts
- Advertising page for my other books/website

My book will include:

_____
_____
_____
_____
_____
_____
_____
_____
_____
_____

Visual Interior Layout

Sketch the interior pages of your book.

Inside Front Cover	Page 1
Page 2	**Page 3**
Page 4	**Page 5**

Visual Interior Layout

Sketch the interior pages of your book.

Page 6	Page 7
Page 8	Page 9
Page 10	Page 11

Visual Interior Layout

Sketch the interior pages of your book.

Page 12	Page 13
Page 14	Page 15
Page 16	Page 17

Visual Interior Layout

Sketch the interior pages of your book.

Page 18	Page 19
Page 20	Page 21
Page 22	Page 23

Visual Interior Layout

Sketch the interior pages of your book.

Page 24	Page 25
Page 26	Page 27
Page 28	Page 29

Back Cover

Use this page to sketch your back cover design.

Front Cover

Use this page to sketch your front cover design.

Congratulations!!

You finished your low content book!

Book #7

As you progress through each step of your book, write down the book details for easy reference.

Book Idea: _____

Date Started: _____

Date Published: _____

File name of interior file: _____

File name of cover file: _____

Title: _____

Size: _____ # Pages: _____

ISBN: _____

Printer: _____

Cost: _____ Selling Price: _____

Primary Font & Size: _____

Secondary Font & Size: _____

Accent Font & Size: _____

Primary Cover Color: _____

Secondary Cover Color: _____

Cover Image Source: _____

Cover Image Credit: _____

Keyword Research

Write down your criteria for validating keywords.
Examples are Monthly Search Volume > 5,000 and Number of Competing Products < 3,000.

Keyword Research

Make a list of the keywords & phrases that you'll be targeting.

Customer Reviews

Read the customer reviews of the competing products. Write down what people liked and didn't like:

What people liked:

1. _____
2. _____
3. _____
4. _____
5. _____
6. _____
7. _____
8. _____
9. _____
10. _____

What people didn't like:

1. _____
2. _____
3. _____
4. _____
5. _____
6. _____
7. _____
8. _____
9. _____
10. _____

Target Audience

My target audience:

_____
_____
_____
_____
_____
_____

Top reason why a member of my target audience will buy and write a 5-star review about my book:

_____
_____
_____
_____
_____
_____

For Bundlers -

What other products is my target audience looking for that will compliment my book?

1. _____
2. _____
3. _____
4. _____
5. _____

Book Details

Language: _____

Title: _____

Subtitle: _____

Series Name: _____ Number: _____

Edition Number: _____

Author: _____

Additional Contributor: _____ Role: _____

Publishing Rights: ❏ I own the copyright   ❏ This is a public domain work

Category 1: _____

Category 2: _____

Adult Content: ❏ Yes   ❏ No

Book Details

Keywords:

_____
_____
_____
_____
_____
_____
_____

Description:

_____
_____
_____
_____
_____
_____
_____
_____
_____
_____
_____
_____
_____

Book Details

Continue your book description, write your back cover description or write additional notes.

_____
_____
_____
_____
_____
_____
_____
_____
_____
_____
_____
_____
_____
_____
_____
_____
_____
_____
_____
_____
_____
_____

Book Details

ISBN: ❑ Free KDP ISBN   ❑ Use my own ISBN

ISBN Number: _____

Publication Date: _____

Print Options: ❑ B & W Interior Cream Paper   ❑ B & W White Paper
                  ❑ Color Interior
                  ❑ Other: _____

Trim Size: _____

Bleed Settings: ❑ No Bleed   ❑ Bleed

Cover Finish: ❑ Matte   ❑ Glossy

List other book details below:

_____
_____
_____
_____
_____
_____
_____

Interior Layout

Think about your book pages and the elements that they will include.

Examples:
- Copyright Page
- Title Page
- Pages with blank lines, dot grids, and doodling boxes.
- Blank recipe pages
- To-Do list with check boxes
- Coloring page with a flower
- Log page with table to record dates and readings
- Daily, weekly, monthly or annual calendar
- Goal-tracking page with an inspirational quote
- Writing prompts
- Advertising page for my other books/website

My book will include:

_____
_____
_____
_____
_____
_____
_____
_____
_____
_____

Visual Interior Layout

Sketch the interior pages of your book.

Inside Front Cover	Page 1
Page 2	**Page 3**
Page 4	**Page 5**

Visual Interior Layout

Sketch the interior pages of your book.

Page 6	Page 7
Page 8	Page 9
Page 10	Page 11

Visual Interior Layout

Sketch the interior pages of your book.

Page 12	Page 13
Page 14	Page 15
Page 16	Page 17

Visual Interior Layout

Sketch the interior pages of your book.

Page 18	Page 19
Page 20	Page 21
Page 22	Page 23

Visual Interior Layout

Sketch the interior pages of your book.

Page 24	Page 25
Page 26	Page 27
Page 28	Page 29

Back Cover

Use this page to sketch your back cover design.

Front Cover

Use this page to sketch your front cover design.

Congratulations!!

You finished your low content book!

Book #8

As you progress through each step of your book, write down the book details for easy reference.

Book Idea: _____

Date Started: _____

Date Published: _____

File name of interior file: _____

File name of cover file: _____

Title: _____

Size: _____ # Pages: _____

ISBN: _____

Printer: _____

Cost: _____ Selling Price: _____

Primary Font & Size: _____

Secondary Font & Size: _____

Accent Font & Size: _____

Primary Cover Color: _____

Secondary Cover Color: _____

Cover Image Source: _____

Cover Image Credit: _____

Keyword Research

Write down your criteria for validating keywords.
Examples are Monthly Search Volume > 5,000 and Number of Competing Products < 3,000.

Keyword Research

Make a list of the keywords & phrases that you'll be targeting.

_____
_____
_____
_____
_____
_____
_____
_____
_____
_____
_____
_____
_____
_____
_____
_____
_____
_____
_____
_____
_____
_____
_____
_____

Customer Reviews

Read the customer reviews of the competing products. Write down what people liked and didn't like:

What people liked:

1. _____
2. _____
3. _____
4. _____
5. _____
6. _____
7. _____
8. _____
9. _____
10. _____

What people didn't like:

1. _____
2. _____
3. _____
4. _____
5. _____
6. _____
7. _____
8. _____
9. _____
10. _____

Target Audience

My target audience:

_____
_____
_____
_____
_____
_____

Top reason why a member of my target audience will buy and write a 5-star review about my book:

_____
_____
_____
_____
_____
_____

For Bundlers -

What other products is my target audience looking for that will compliment my book?

1. _____
2. _____
3. _____
4. _____
5. _____

Book Details

Language: _____

Title: _____

Subtitle: _____

Series Name: _____ Number: _____

Edition Number: _____

Author: _____

Additional Contributor: _____ Role: _____

Publishing Rights: ❏ I own the copyright   ❏ This is a public domain work

Category 1: _____

Category 2: _____

Adult Content: ❏ Yes   ❏ No

Book Details

Keywords:

_____
_____
_____
_____
_____
_____
_____

Description:

_____
_____
_____
_____
_____
_____
_____
_____
_____
_____
_____
_____
_____
_____

Book Details

Continue your book description, write your back cover description or write additional notes.

Book Details

ISBN: ❑ Free KDP ISBN   ❑ Use my own ISBN

ISBN Number: _____

Publication Date: _____

Print Options: ❑ B & W Interior Cream Paper   ❑ B & W White Paper
       ❑ Color Interior
       ❑ Other: _____

Trim Size: _____

Bleed Settings: ❑ No Bleed   ❑ Bleed

Cover Finish: ❑ Matte   ❑ Glossy

List other book details below:

_____
_____
_____
_____
_____
_____
_____

Interior Layout

Think about your book pages and the elements that they will include.

Examples:
- Copyright Page
- Title Page
- Pages with blank lines, dot grids, and doodling boxes.
- Blank recipe pages
- To-Do list with check boxes
- Coloring page with a flower
- Log page with table to record dates and readings
- Daily, weekly, monthly or annual calendar
- Goal-tracking page with an inspirational quote
- Writing prompts
- Advertising page for my other books/website

My book will include:

_____
_____
_____
_____
_____
_____
_____
_____
_____

Visual Interior Layout

Sketch the interior pages of your book.

Inside Front Cover	Page 1
Page 2	**Page 3**
Page 4	**Page 5**

Visual Interior Layout

Sketch the interior pages of your book.

Page 6	Page 7
Page 8	Page 9
Page 10	Page 11

Visual Interior Layout

Sketch the interior pages of your book.

Page 12	Page 13
Page 14	Page 15
Page 16	Page 17

Visual Interior Layout

Sketch the interior pages of your book.

Page 18	Page 19
Page 20	Page 21
Page 22	Page 23

Visual Interior Layout

Sketch the interior pages of your book.

Page 24	Page 25
Page 26	Page 27
Page 28	Page 29

Back Cover

Use this page to sketch your back cover design.

Front Cover

Use this page to sketch your front cover design.

Congratulations!!

You finished your low content book!

Book #9

As you progress through each step of your book, write down the book details for easy reference.

Book Idea: _____

Date Started: _____

Date Published: _____

File name of interior file: _____

File name of cover file: _____

Title: _____

Size: _____ # Pages: _____

ISBN: _____

Printer: _____

Cost: _____ Selling Price: _____

Primary Font & Size: _____

Secondary Font & Size: _____

Accent Font & Size: _____

Primary Cover Color: _____

Secondary Cover Color: _____

Cover Image Source: _____

Cover Image Credit: _____

Keyword Research

Write down your criteria for validating keywords.
Examples are Monthly Search Volume > 5,000 and Number of Competing Products < 3,000.

Keyword Research

Make a list of the keywords & phrases that you'll be targeting.

_____
_____
_____
_____
_____
_____
_____
_____
_____
_____
_____
_____
_____
_____
_____
_____
_____
_____
_____
_____
_____
_____
_____
_____

Customer Reviews

Read the customer reviews of the competing products. Write down what people liked and didn't like:

What people liked:

1. _____
2. _____
3. _____
4. _____
5. _____
6. _____
7. _____
8. _____
9. _____
10. _____

What people didn't like:

1. _____
2. _____
3. _____
4. _____
5. _____
6. _____
7. _____
8. _____
9. _____
10. _____

Target Audience

My target audience:

_____
_____
_____
_____
_____
_____

Top reason why a member of my target audience will buy and write a 5-star review about my book:

_____
_____
_____
_____
_____
_____

For Bundlers -

What other products is my target audience looking for that will compliment my book?

1. _____
2. _____
3. _____
4. _____
5. _____

Book Details

Language: _____

Title: _____

Subtitle: _____

Series Name: _____ Number: _____

Edition Number: _____

Author: _____

Additional Contributor: _____ Role: _____

Publishing Rights: ❑ I own the copyright   ❑ This is a public domain work

Category 1: _____

Category 2: _____

Adult Content: ❑ Yes   ❑ No

Book Details

Keywords:

Description:

Book Details

Continue your book description, write your back cover description or write additional notes.

Book Details

ISBN: ❑ Free KDP ISBN ❑ Use my own ISBN

ISBN Number: _____

Publication Date: _____

Print Options: ❑ B & W Interior Cream Paper ❑ B & W White Paper
 ❑ Color Interior
 ❑ Other: _____

Trim Size:_____

Bleed Settings: ❑ No Bleed ❑ Bleed

Cover Finish: ❑ Matte ❑ Glossy

List other book details below:

_____
_____
_____
_____
_____
_____
_____

Interior Layout

Think about your book pages and the elements that they will include.

Examples:
- Copyright Page
- Title Page
- Pages with blank lines, dot grids, and doodling boxes.
- Blank recipe pages
- To-Do list with check boxes
- Coloring page with a flower
- Log page with table to record dates and readings
- Daily, weekly, monthly or annual calendar
- Goal-tracking page with an inspirational quote
- Writing prompts
- Advertising page for my other books/website

My book will include:

_____
_____
_____
_____
_____
_____
_____
_____
_____
_____

Visual Interior Layout

Sketch the interior pages of your book.

Inside Front Cover	**Page 1**
Page 2	**Page 3**
Page 4	**Page 5**

Visual Interior Layout

Sketch the interior pages of your book.

Page 6	**Page 7**
Page 8	**Page 9**
Page 10	**Page 11**

Visual Interior Layout

Sketch the interior pages of your book.

Page 12	Page 13
Page 14	Page 15
Page 16	Page 17

Visual Interior Layout

Sketch the interior pages of your book.

Page 18	Page 19
Page 20	Page 21
Page 22	Page 23

Visual Interior Layout

Sketch the interior pages of your book.

Page 24	Page 25
Page 26	Page 27
Page 28	Page 29

Back Cover

Use this page to sketch your back cover design.

Front Cover

Use this page to sketch your front cover design.

Congratulations!!

You finished your low content book!

Book #10

As you progress through each step of your book, write down the book details for easy reference.

Book Idea: _____

Date Started: _____

Date Published: _____

File name of interior file: _____

File name of cover file: _____

Title: _____

Size: _____ # Pages: _____

ISBN: _____

Printer: _____

Cost: _____ Selling Price: _____

Primary Font & Size: _____

Secondary Font & Size: _____

Accent Font & Size: _____

Primary Cover Color: _____

Secondary Cover Color: _____

Cover Image Source: _____

Cover Image Credit: _____

Keyword Research

Write down your criteria for validating keywords.
Examples are Monthly Search Volume > 5,000 and Number of Competing Products < 3,000.

Keyword Research

Make a list of the keywords & phrases that you'll be targeting.

Customer Reviews

Read the customer reviews of the competing products. Write down what people liked and didn't like:

What people liked:

1. _____
2. _____
3. _____
4. _____
5. _____
6. _____
7. _____
8. _____
9. _____
10. _____

What people didn't like:

1. _____
2. _____
3. _____
4. _____
5. _____
6. _____
7. _____
8. _____
9. _____
10. _____

Target Audience

My target audience:

_____
_____
_____
_____
_____
_____

Top reason why a member of my target audience will buy and write a 5-star review about my book:

_____
_____
_____
_____
_____
_____

For Bundlers -

What other products is my target audience looking for that will compliment my book?

1. _____
2. _____
3. _____
4. _____
5. _____

Book Details

Language: _____

Title: _____

Subtitle: _____

Series Name: _____ Number: _____

Edition Number: _____

Author: _____

Additional Contributor: _____ Role: _____

Publishing Rights: ❏ I own the copyright   ❏ This is a public domain work

Category 1: _____

Category 2: _____

Adult Content: ❏ Yes   ❏ No

Book Details

Keywords:

Description:

Book Details

Continue your book description, write your back cover description or write additional notes.

Book Details

ISBN: ❏ Free KDP ISBN   ❏ Use my own ISBN

ISBN Number: _____

Publication Date: _____

Print Options: ❏ B & W Interior Cream Paper   ❏ B & W White Paper
                 ❏ Color Interior
                 ❏ Other: _____

Trim Size: _____

Bleed Settings: ❏ No Bleed   ❏ Bleed

Cover Finish: ❏ Matte   ❏ Glossy

List other book details below:

_____
_____
_____
_____
_____
_____
_____

Interior Layout

Think about your book pages and the elements that they will include.

Examples:
- Copyright Page
- Title Page
- Pages with blank lines, dot grids, and doodling boxes.
- Blank recipe pages
- To-Do list with check boxes
- Coloring page with a flower
- Log page with table to record dates and readings
- Daily, weekly, monthly or annual calendar
- Goal-tracking page with an inspirational quote
- Writing prompts
- Advertising page for my other books/website

My book will include:

_____
_____
_____
_____
_____
_____
_____
_____
_____

Visual Interior Layout

Sketch the interior pages of your book.

Inside Front Cover	Page 1
Page 2	**Page 3**
Page 4	**Page 5**

Visual Interior Layout

Sketch the interior pages of your book.

Page 6	Page 7
Page 8	Page 9
Page 10	Page 11

Visual Interior Layout

Sketch the interior pages of your book.

Page 12	Page 13
Page 14	Page 15
Page 16	Page 17

Visual Interior Layout

Sketch the interior pages of your book.

Page 18	Page 19
Page 20	Page 21
Page 22	Page 23

Visual Interior Layout

Sketch the interior pages of your book.

Page 24	**Page 25**
Page 26	**Page 27**
Page 28	**Page 29**

Back Cover

Use this page to sketch your back cover design.

Front Cover

Use this page to sketch your front cover design.

Congratulations!!

You finished your low content book!

Made in United States
Orlando, FL
02 June 2023